the **Shih Tzu**

A guide to selection, care, nutrition,

upbringing, training, health, breeding,

sports and play

Contents

Foreword

The book you are holding is not intended to be a complete 'owners' manual' for the Shih Tzu. If we had tried to cover all the information available about this breed, its history and development, feeding, training, health, ailments and whatever more, this would be a book of at least 500 pages.

What we have done however, is to collect basic information to help the (future) owner of a Shih Tzu look after his or her pet responsibly. Too many people still buy a pet before really understanding what they're about to get into.

This book goes into the broad history of the Shih Tzu, the breed standard and some pros and cons of buying a Shih Tzu. You will also find essential information on feeding, initial training and an introduction into canine reproduction. Finally we pay attention to (day-by-day) care, health and some breed-specific ailments.

Based on this information, you can buy a Shih Tzu, having thought it through carefully, and keep it as a pet in a responsible manner. Our advice, though, is not just to leave it to this small book. A properly brought-up and well-trained dog is more than just a dog. Invest a little extra in a puppy training course or an obedience course. There are also excellent books available that go deeper into certain aspects than is possible here.

About Pets

A Publication of About Pets.

Copyright © 2005
About Pets
co-publisher United Kingdom
Kingdom Books
PO9 5TL, England

ISBN 1852792312
First printing September 2005

Original title: *de Shih Tzu*
© 1999 - 2005 Welzo Media Productions bv,
About Pets bv
Warffum, the Netherlands
www.aboutpets.info

Editor: Miroslaw Redlicki

Photos:
Sylvia van der Meer, Isabelle Francais,, Rob
Dekker, Kingdom Books, WMP,

Printed in China through Printworks Int.Ltd.

In general

The Shih Tzu is an eye-catching and charming companion dog of sweet disposition and full of mischief. Its long coat, when left in natural length, requires a considerable amount of grooming if it is to look nice.

First and foremost a companion dog, the Shih Tzu thrives on human affection and companionship.

Origins

The origins of the Shih Tzu remain rather mysterious. It is known that the breed originated in Tibet, yet it is impossible to establish exactly when this happened. Dogs have always been highly valued in the Tibetan society and religion, having been bred in monasteries and palaces, as well as in remote villages. They have enjoyed good treatment and human affection. Due to close relations between Tibet and the Chinese Empire, Tibetan dogs found their way to the Imperial Palace in Beijing.

Here they were kept in large numbers at least since the early days of the Manchu (Ching) Dynasty in the 17th century. Strict rules were applied to both the general care and breeding, which aimed at the smallest possible size and the greatest possible similarity to a miniature lion. Dog breeding in the Palace came to its climax during the reign of Emperor Tao Kung and the Empress Dowager – Tzu His (who died 1908). She personally supervised several hundred dogs; some of them were classified as the Tibetan strain and were distinctly different to the already established Pekingese. Their heads were longer and the coat was long and shaggy with a slight wave. After the Empress Dowager's death, the Imperial

kennels were grossly reduced and abandoned at the time of Revolution (1924). Some dogs, however, went to private homes. Several of those so-called "Tibetan Lion Dogs" were eventually exhibited at Peking dog shows. The Breed Club was formed and the breed standard written by a French resident, Countess D'Anjou, in 1933.

Meanwhile the first pair of Shih Tzu was brought to Great Britain by Lady Brownrigg upon her returning to the country, which was to become the breed's new homeland. That original pair, together with dogs brought into Norway by a Mrs Kauffmann, formed the foundations of modern breeding outside China. The British Club was established by Lady Brownrigg, who was loyal to this breed for more than thirty years. The Shih Tzu gained popularity in the sixties and nowadays it is one of the most popular companion dogs worldwide.

Characteristics
Even though the Shih Tzu is a small dog, it is sturdy, tough and mentally stable. It is full of itself and behaves as if it was much bigger than it actually is. As the sole purpose of this breed has always been that of a companion and a pet, this dog is never nervous or shy; it is not supposed to be noisy, either. Apart from the time-consuming grooming, it is one of the best pet dogs you can find. It is good with children, who should be told well in advance that they must not be too rough with it. The Shih Tzu is kind to other domestic pets and should be kept indoors, never outdoors. It needs constant attention and human companionship.

General appearance

One who happens to see a well-groomed shih tzu will agree that it is a dog of great beauty. It moves with smooth, free, ground-covering stride, head carried proudly and high as if it was looking at the world from above. The standard describes this attitude as distinctly arrogant, yet it can be better regarded as being full of itself. Its unique expression comes from a short, broad muzzle, large eyes and a domed skull. The Shih Tzu is small, but it is sturdily built and heavily boned. Its body is slightly longer than its height, its ribcage is broad, and the tail is curled gaily over the back, well covered with abundant hair and in the form of a plume. The whole body, including the head, is well covered with long hair. On the head it is neatly tied up to form a so-called "topknot". Although this long coat adds to the dog's natural beauty, it can be clipped for convenience. The clipped adult dog resembles a big puppy.

UK Kennel Club and the breed standard

What does the UK Kennel Club do?

To put it in their own words: "The Kennel Club is committed to developing and supporting a nation of responsible dog owners. As well as organising

events and campaigns to help dog owners meet their responsibilities, the Kennel Club also produces a range of literature to assist the dog-owning public."
What is the use of a Breed Standard?
The Kennel Club answers: "The basis of breed shows is the judging of dogs against the 'Breed Standard', which is the prescribed blueprint of the particular breed of dog. For all licensed breed shows, the Kennel Club Breed Standards must be used for the judging of dogs."
More about the UK Kennel Club Breed Standards: "The Breed Standards are owned by the Kennel Club, and all changes are subject to approval by the Kennel Club General Committee. New Breed Standards, for newly recognised breeds, are drawn up once the breed has become sufficiently established within the UK. Careful research is conducted into the historical background, health and temperament of any new breed before Kennel Club recognition is granted. The Kennel Club currently recognises 196 breeds. Upon recognition, breeds are placed on the Imported Breed Register until they are deemed eligible for transferral to the Breed Register".
A standard provides a guideline

for breeders and judges. It is something of an ideal that dogs of any breed must strive to match. With some breeds, dogs are already being bred that match the ideal. Other breeds have a long way to go. There is a list of defects for each breed. These can be serious defects that disqualify a dog, in which case it will be excluded from breeding. Permitted defects are not serious, but do cost points in a show.

The Shih Tzu is listed in the utility group. Miscellaneous breeds join the Shih Tzu in this group. They are mainly of a non-sporting origin, such as the Bulldog, Dalmatian, Japanese Akita and Poodle. Some breeds listed in the utility group belong to the oldest documented dog breeds in the world and the group displays extreme variety. Most breeds were selectively bred for a specific function and do therefore not fit in the sporting and working categories.

The UK Kennel Club Breed Standard for the Shih Tzu

General Appearance
Sturdy, abundantly coated dog with distinctly arrogant carriage and chrysanthemum-like face.

Characteristics
Intelligent, active and alert.

Temperament
Friendly and independent.

Head and Skull
Head broad, round, wide between eyes. Shock-headed with hair falling well over eyes. Good beard and whiskers, hair growing upwards on the nose giving a distinctly chrysanthemum-like effect. Muzzle of ample width, square, short, not wrinkled; flat and hairy. Nose black but dark liver in liver or liver marked dogs and about one inch from tip to definite stop. Nose level or slightly tip-tilted. Top of nose

leather should be on a line with or slightly below lower eye rim. Wide-open nostrils. Down-pointed nose highly undesirable, as are pinched nostrils. Pigmentation of muzzle as unbroken as possible.

Eyes
Large, dark, round, placed well apart but not prominent. Warm expression. In liver or liver-marked dogs, lighter eye colour permissible. No white of eye showing.

Ears
Large, with long leathers, carried drooping. Set slightly below crown of skull, so heavily coated they appear to blend into hair of neck.

Mouth
Wide, slightly undershot or level. Lips level.

Neck
Well proportioned, nicely arched. Sufficient length to carry head proudly.

Forequarters
Shoulders well laid back. Legs short and muscular with ample bone, as straight as possible, consistent with broad chest being well let down.

Body
Longer between withers and root of tail than height of withers, well coupled and sturdy, chest broad and deep, shoulders firm, back level.

Hindquarters
Legs short and muscular with ample bone. Straight when viewed from the rear. Thighs well rounded and muscular. Legs looking massive on account of wealth of hair.

Feet
Rounded, firm and well padded, appearing big on account of wealth of hair.

Tail
Heavily plumed, carried gaily well over back. Set on high. Height approximately level with that of skull to give a balanced outline.

Gait/Movement
Arrogant, smooth-flowing, front legs reaching well forward, strong rear action and showing full pad.

Coat
Long, dense, not curly, with good undercoat. Slight wave permitted. Strongly recommended that hair on head tied up.

Colour
All colours permissible, white blaze on forehead and white tip to tail highly desirable in parti-colours.

Size
Height at withers not more than 27 cms (10 1/2 ins), type and breed characteristics of the utmost importance and on no account to be sacrificed to size alone. Weight: 4.5-8 kgs (10-18 lbs). Ideal weight 4.5-7.5 kgs (10-16 lbs).

Faults
Any departure from the foregoing points should be considered a fault and the seriousness with which the fault should be regarded should be in exact proportion to its degree and its effect upon the health and welfare of the dog.

Note
Male animals should have two apparently normal testicles fully descended into the scrotum.
Courtesy of the Kennel Club UK September 2000

Buying a Shih Tzu

Once you've made that properly considered decision to buy a dog, there are several options. Should it be a puppy, an adult dog, or even an older dog? Should it be a bitch or a male dog, a pedigree dog or a cross?

Are you looking for a companion or a real show dog? Of course, the question also comes up as to where to buy your dog. Are you going to buy it from a private person, a reliable breeder, or would you maybe even get it from an animal asylum? It is important for you and the animal that you sort out these things in advance. You want to find a dog that fits in with your situation. With a puppy, you choose a playful, energetic housemate, which will adapt easily to its new surroundings. If you want something a little quieter, an older dog is a good choice.

Advantages and disadvantages
The long coat of this breed needs plenty of care every day. This can be both an advantage and a disadvantage. Some people do not enjoy spending a lot of time grooming their dog, whereas others particularly enjoy making their dog as beautiful as possible. A well cared for Shih Tzu will get everybody's attention.

The Shih Tzu has an undercoat. This means that they have a moulting period, and they need a lot of attention when it comes to grooming. An advantage is that these dogs have no problems keeping themselves warm and that they don't need any extra protection when it gets cold.

These dogs are very small and they fit into any house. This is, of course, an advantage. They don't need very much exercise, but it is better for them if they build up a good condition. This breed is very focused on its master and loves to be with him as much as possible. They will follow you around all day long. Both visitors and the postman are greeted with loud barking. A Shih Tzu becomes approximately twelve years old.

Male or female?

Whether you choose a male or a female puppy, or an adult dog or bitch, is an entirely personal decision. With the Shih Tzu, the difference in character between a male and a bitch is also not that great. Males are often reproached for urinating everywhere, being dominant, disobedient and running away. These problems have more to do with their upbringing than their nature. Bitches are often assumed to be more affectionate, but for a real cuddle you need to look among the males. The male is also somewhat more tolerant by nature. When a bitch has had enough, the male will simply lift his head and get up and go for the next round. Many males are more spontaneous and affectionate than bitches.

A male is usually more sturdy and ample in format. Naturally they want to set their own scent in places, but with your dog on the lead, you're in charge, aren't you? And once they've set their first mark, their urgent need is taken care of. With a Shih Tzu, you also don't need to worry that it becomes too heavy to pull if necessary. You can also teach them to urinate only once or twice each time they go out on the lead.

A puppy test is good for defining what kind of character a young dog will develop. During such a test one usually sees that a dog is more dominant than a bitch. You can often quickly recognise the bossy, the adventurous and the cautious characters. So visit the litter a couple of times early on.

Particularly in the second half of her season, she will want to go looking for a dog to mate with. A male dog will show more masculine traits once he is sexually mature. He will make sure other dogs know what territory is his by urinating as often as possible in as many places as he can. He is also difficult to restrain if there's a bitch in season nearby. As far as normal care is concerned there is little difference between a dog and a bitch.

Puppy or adult?

After you've made the decision for a male or female, the next question comes up. Should it be a puppy or an adult dog? Your household circumstances usually play a major role here.

Try to pick a puppy that suits your own personality. A dominant dog, for instance, needs a strong hand. It will often try to see how far it can go. You must regularly make clear who's the boss, and that it must obey all the members of the family.

When bitches are sexually mature, they will go into season. On average, a bitch is in season twice a year for about two or three weeks. This is the fertile period when she can become pregnant.

Of course, it's great having a sweet little puppy in the house, but bringing up a young dog takes a lot of time. In the first year of its life it learns more than during the rest of its life. This is the period when the foundations are laid for elementary matters such as house-training, obedience and social behaviour. You must reckon with the fact that your puppy will keep you busy for a couple of hours a day, certainly in the first few months. You won't need so much time with a grown dog. It has already been brought up, but this doesn't mean it won't need correcting from time to time.

A puppy will no doubt leave a trail of destruction in its wake for the first few months. With a little bad luck, this will cost you a number of rolls of wallpaper, some good shoes and a few socks. In the worst case you'll be left with some chewed furniture. Some puppies even manage to tear curtains from their rails. With good upbringing this 'vandalism' will quickly disappear, but you won't have to worry about this if you get an older dog.

The greatest advantage of a puppy, of course, is that you can bring it up your own way. The upbringing a dog receives (or not) is of major influence on its whole character. Finally, financial aspects may play a role in your choice. A puppy is generally (much) more expensive than an adult dog, not only in purchase price but also in 'maintenance'. A puppy needs to go to the vet's more often for the necessary vaccinations and check-ups.

Overall, bringing up a puppy requires a good deal of energy, time and money, but you have its upbringing in your own hands. An adult dog requiers less money and time, but its character is already formed. You should also try to find out about the background of an adult dog. Its previous owner may have formed its character in somewhat less positive ways.

Ten golden puppy rules
- Walk your puppy in doses followed by one hour play, a feed and then three hours sleep.
- Don't let your puppy run endlessly after a ball or stick.
- Don't let your puppy romp wildly with large, heavy dogs.
- Never let your puppy play with a full tummy.
- Don't give your puppy anything to drink straight after a meal.
- Don't let your puppy walk up and down steps for the first year. Be careful with shiny floors.
- Don't add supplements to ready-made food.
- Watch out for your puppy's weight. Being overweight can lead to bone abnormalities.
- Give your puppy a quiet place to sleep.
- Pick your puppy up carefully, one hand under its chest, the other under its hindquarters.

Two dogs?

Having two or more dogs in the house is not just nice for us, but also for the animals themselves. Dogs get a lot of pleasure from each others' company. After all, they are pack animals.

If you're sure that you want two young dogs, it's best not to buy them at the same time. Bringing up a dog and establishing the bond between dog and master takes time, and you need to give a lot of attention to your dog during this phase. Having two puppies in the house means that you have to divide your attention between them. Apart from that, there's a danger that they will focus on one another rather than on their master. Buy the second pup when the first is (almost) an adult.

Two adult dogs can happily be brought into the home together, as long as they're used to each other. If this is not the case, then they have to go through that process. This is usually best achieved by letting them get to know each other on neutral territory. This prevents fights for territory. On neutral territory, perhaps an acquaintance's garden where neither dog has been before, both dogs are basically equal. Once they've got to know each other, you can take them both home, and they can sort out the hierarchy there amongst themselves. In any event, don't get involved in trying

to 'arbitrate'. That is human, but for the dog at the top of the pecking order it's like having its position undone. It will only make the dog more dominant in behaviour, with all the consequences. Once the hierarchy is established, most dogs can get along fine together. Luckily, Shih Tzu do not tend to be fighters and enjoy the company of other dogs of their own breed.

Getting a puppy when the first dog is somewhat older often has a positive effect on the older dog. The influence of the puppy almost seems to give it a second childhood. The older dog, if it's been well brought up, can help with the upbringing of the puppy. Young dogs like to imitate the behaviour of their elders. Don't forget to give both dogs the same amount of attention. Take both out alone at least once per day during the first eighteen months. Give the older dog enough opportunity to get some peace and quiet. It won't want an enthusiastic youngster running around under its feet all the time. Moreover, a puppy needs plenty of sleep and may have to have the brakes put on it once in a while.

The combination of male and female needs special attention whatever the breed, and so also in the case of the Shih Tzu. It's advisable to get a second dog of the same sex. This will avoid a lot

A dog isn't comfortable when it's messed around with. It can become frightened, timid and even aggressive. So make it clear what a dog likes and what not. With the Shih Tzu, it's important to make sure the dog doesn't accept too much. Look for ways the child can play with the dog, perhaps a game of hide and seek where the child hides and the dog has to find it. Even a simple tennis ball can give enormous pleasure. Children must learn to leave a dog in peace when it doesn't want to play any more. The dog must also have its own place where it's not disturbed. Have children help with your dog's care as much as possible. A strong bond will be the result.

of problems. Sterilisation or castration is, of course, one solution, but it's a final one. A sterilised or castrated animal can never reproduce. Additionally, sterilisation or castration can lead to abundant hair growth, which usually means a thicker, duller and softer coat, which is difficult to groom.

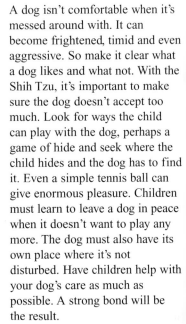

A dog and children

Dogs and children are a great combination. They can play together and get great pleasure out of each other's company. Moreover, children need to learn how to handle living beings; they develop respect and a sense of responsibility by caring for a dog (or other pets). However sweet a dog is, children must understand that it is an animal and not a toy.

The arrival of a baby also means changes in the life of a dog. Before the birth you can help get your dog acquainted with the new situation. Let it sniff at the new things in the house and it will quickly accept them. When the baby has arrived involve the dog as much as possible in day-by-day events, but make sure it gets plenty of attention too. NEVER leave a dog alone with young children. Crawling infants sometimes make unexpected movements, which can easily frighten a dog. Infants are also hugely curious, and may try to find out whether the tail is really fastened to the dog, or whether its eyes come out, just like they do with their cuddly toys. A dog is always just a dog and it will defend itself when it feels threatened.

Where to buy

There are various ways to acquire a dog. The decision for a puppy or an adult dog will also define for the most part where to buy your dog.

If it's to be a puppy, then you need to find a breeder with a litter. If you chose a popular breed like the Shih Tzu, there is choice enough. You may also face the problem that there are so many puppies on sale that have only been bred for profit's sake. You can see how many puppies are for sale by looking in the regional newspaper every Saturday. Some of these dogs have a pedigree, but many don't. Breeders often don't watch out for breed-specific illnesses and inbreeding; puppies are separated from their mother as fast as possible and are thus insufficiently socialised. Never buy a puppy that is too young, or whose mother you weren't able to see.

Fortunately, there are also enough bona-fide breeders of Shih Tzu. Try to visit a number of breeders before you actually buy your puppy. Ask if the breeder is prepared to help you after you've bought your puppy, and to help you find solutions for any problems that may come up.

Things to watch out for

Buying a puppy is no simple matter. You must pay attention to the following:

- Never buy a puppy on impulse, even if it is love at first sight. A dog is a living being that will need care and attention over a long period. It is not a toy that you can put away when you're done with it.
- Take a good look at the mother. Is she calm, nervous, aggressive, well cared for or neglected? The behaviour and condition of the mother is not only a sign of the quality of the breeder, but also of the puppy you're about to buy.
- Avoid buying a puppy whose mother has been kept only in a kennel. A young dog needs as many different impressions as possible in its first few months, including living in a family group. This helps it get used to people and possibly other pets. Kennel dogs miss these experiences and are inadequately socialised.
- Always ask to see the parents' papers (vaccination certificates, pedigrees, official reports of health examinations).
- Never buy a puppy younger than eight weeks.
- Put all agreements with the breeder in writing. A model agreement is available from the breed association.

If you're looking for an adult dog, it's best to contact the breed association among others, who often help rehome adult dogs that can no longer be kept by their owners because of personal circumstances (impulse buying, moving home, divorce etc.).

Finally, you must realise that a pedigree is nothing more or less than a proof of descent. The Kennel Club also issues pedigrees to the young of parents that suffer from a congenital condition, or that have never been checked for them. A pedigree says nothing about the health of the parent dogs or of your puppy.

Travelling with your Shih Tzu

There are a few things to think about before travelling with your dog. While one dog may enjoy travelling, another may hate it.

You may like holidays in far-away places, but it's questionable whether your dog will enjoy them as much.

That very first trip

The first trip of a puppy's life is also the most nerve-wrecking. This is the trip from the breeder's to its new home. If possible, pick up your puppy in the morning. It then has the whole day to get used to the new situation. Ask the breeder not to feed it that day. The young animal will be overwhelmed by all kinds of new experiences. Firstly, it's away from its mother; it's in a small room (the car) with all its different smells, noises and strange people. So there's a big chance that the puppy will be car-sick this first time, with the annoying consequence that it will remember travelling in the car as an unpleasant experience.

So it's important to make this first trip as pleasant as possible. When picking up a puppy, always take someone with you who can sit in the back seat with the puppy on his or her lap and talk to it calmly. If it's too warm for the puppy, a place on the floor at the feet of your companion is ideal. The pup will lie there relatively quietly and may even take a nap. Ask the breeder for a cloth or something else from its nest that carries a familiar scent. The puppy can lie on this in the car, and it will also help if it feels alone during the first nights at home.

If the trip home is a long one, then stop for a break (once in a while). Let your puppy roam and sniff around (on the lead!), have a little drink and, if necessary, let it do its business. Do take care to lay an old towel in the car. It can happen that the puppy, in its nervousness, may urinate or be sick. It's also good advice to give a puppy positive experiences with car journeys. Make short trips to nice places where you can walk and play with it. It can be a real nuisance if your dog doesn't like travelling in a car. After all, once in a while you will have to take it to certain places, such as the vet's or to visit friends and acquaintances.

Taking your Shih Tzu on holiday

When making holiday plans, you also need to think about what you're going to do with your dog during that time. Are you taking it with you, putting it into kennels or leaving it with friends? In any event there are a number of things you need to do in good time. If you want to take your dog with you, you need to be sure in advance that it will be welcome at your holiday home, and what the rules there are. If you're going abroad it will need certain vaccinations, perhaps even blood tests, and a health certificate, which normally need to be done some time before departure. You must also be sure that you've

made all the arrangements necessary to bring your dog back home to the UK, without it needing to go into quarantine under the rabies regulations. Your vet can give you the most recent information.

If your trip is to southern Europe, ask for a treatment against ticks (you can read more about this in the Parasites chapter).

It can get very hot inside, even with fatal consequences to the dog. If you can't avoid it, park the car in the shade if at all possible, and leave a window open for a little fresh air. Even if you've taken these precautions, never stay away long!

If you're travelling by plane or ship, make sure in good time that your dog can travel with you and what rules you need to observe. You will need some time to make all the arrangements. Maybe you decide not to take your dog with you, and you then need to find somewhere for it to stay. Arrangements for a place in boarding kennels need to be made well in advance, and there may be certain vaccinations required, which need to be given a minimum of one month before the stay.

Although dog-owners usually enjoy taking their dogs on holidays, you must seriously ask yourself whether the dog feels that way too. With its short muzzle and nose, a Shih Tzu certainly doesn't always feel comfortable in a hot country. Days spent travelling in a car are also often not their preference, especially if they suffer badly from car-sickness. There are good medicines for this, but it's questionable whether you're doing your dog a favour with them. If you do decide to take it with you, make regular stops at safe places during your journey, so that your dog can have a good run. Take plenty of fresh drinking water with you, as well as the food your dog is used to. Don't leave your dog in the car standing in the sun.

If your dog can't be accommodated in the homes of relatives or friends, it might be possible to have an acquaintance stay in your house. This also needs to be arranged well in advance, as it may be difficult to find someone who can do this.

Always ensure that your dog can be traced should it run away or get lost while on holiday. A little tube with your address or a tag with home and holiday address can avoid a lot of problems.

Moving home

Dogs generally become more attached to humans than to the house they live in. Moving home is usually not a problem for them. It can be useful before moving to let the dog get to know its new home and the area around it.

If you can, leave your dog with relatives or friends (or in kennels) on the day of the move. The chance of it running away or getting lost is then practically non-existent. When your move is complete, you can pick your dog up and let it quietly get familiar with its new home and environment. Give it its own place in the house at once and it will quickly adapt. During the first week or so, always walk your dog on a lead because an animal can also get lost in new surroundings. Always take a different route so it quickly gets to know the neighbourhood.

Don't forget to get your new address and phone number engraved on the dog's tag. Send a change of address notice to the institution that has any chip or tattoo data. Dogs must sometimes be registered in a new community, and you must pay for a dog licence.

Feeding your Shih Tzu

A dog will eat a lot more than just meat. In the wild it would eat its prey complete with skin and fur, including the bones, stomach, and the innards with their semi-digested vegetable material.

In this way the dog supplements its meat menu with the vitamins and minerals it needs. This is also the basis for feeding a domestic dog.

Ready-made foods
It's not easy for a layman to put together a complete menu for a dog, with all the necessary proteins, fats, vitamins and minerals in just the right proportions and quantities. Meat alone is certainly not a complete meal for a dog. It contains too little calcium. A calcium deficiency will lead to bone defects over time, and for a fast-growing puppy this can lead to serious skeletal deformities.

If you put its food together yourself, you can easily give your dog too much in terms of vitamins and minerals, which can also be bad for your dog's health. You can avoid these problems by giving it ready-made food of a good brand. These products are well-balanced and contain everything your dog needs. Supplements such as vitamin preparations are superfluous. The amount of food your dog needs depends on its weight and activity level. You can find guidelines on the packaging. Split the food into two meals per day if possible, and always ensure there's a dish of fresh drinking water next to its food.

Give your dog the time to digest its food; don't let it outdoors straight after a meal. A dog should also never play with a full stomach.

Because a dog's food needs depend, among other things, on its age and way of life, there are many different types of dog food available. There are "light" foods for less active dogs, "energy" foods for working dogs and "senior" foods for older dogs.

Canned foods, mixers and dry foods

Ready-made foods available at pet shops or in the supermarket can roughly be split into canned food, mixer and dry food. Whichever form you choose, ensure that it's a complete food with all the necessary ingredients. You can see this on the packaging.

Most dogs love canned food. Although the better brands are composed well, they do have one disadvantage: they are soft. A dog fed only on canned food will sooner or later have problems with its teeth (tartar, parodontosis). Apart from canned food, give your dog some hard food at certain times or a dog chew.

Mixer is a food consisting of chunks, dried vegetables and grains. Almost all moisture has been extracted. The advantages of mixer are that it is light and keeps

well. You add a certain amount of water and the meal is ready. A disadvantage is that it must definitely not be fed without water. Without the extra fluid, mixer will absorb the fluids present in the stomach, with serious consequences. Should your dog manage to get at the bag and enjoy its contents, you must immediately give it plenty to drink in small doses. Mixer, prepared with an adequate amount of water, is quite soft; it moistens and stains the dog's beard and moustache.

Dry chunks have also had the moisture extracted but not as much as mixer. The advantage of dry foods is that they are hard, forcing the dog to use its jaws, removing tartar and massaging the gums.

Dog chew products

Naturally, once in a while you want to spoil your dog with something extra. Don't give it pieces of cheese or sausage as these contain too much salt and fat. There are various products available that a dog will find delicious and which are also healthy, especially for its teeth. You'll find a large range of varying quality in your local pet shop.

The butcher's leftovers

The bones of slaughtered animals have traditionally been given to the dog, and dogs are crazy about them, but they are not without risks. Pork and poultry bones are too weak. They can splinter and cause serious injury to the intestines. Beef bones are more

suitable, but they must be cooked first to kill off dangerous bacteria. Pet shops carry a range of smoked, cooked and dried abattoir residue, such as pigs' ears, bull penis, tripe sticks, oxtails, gullet, dried muscle meat, and hoof chews.

Fresh meat

If you do want to give your dog fresh meat occasionally, never give it raw, but always boiled or roasted. Raw (or not fully cooked) pork or chicken can contain life-threatening bacteria. Chicken can be contaminated with the notorious salmonella bacteria, while pork can carry the Aujeszky virus. This disease is incurable and will quickly lead to the death of your pet.

Buffalo or cowhide chews

Dog chews are mostly made of beef or buffalo hide. Chews are usually knotted or pressed hide. Your dog can enjoy many different shapes, such as little shoes, twisted sticks, balls and various other shapes; they are nice to look at and a nice change.

Munchy sticks

Munchy sticks are green, yellow, red or brown coloured sticks of various thicknesses. They consist of ground buffalo hide with a number of often undefined additives. Dogs usually love them because these sticks have been dipped in the blood of slaughtered animals. The composition and quality of these between-meal treats is not always clear. Some are fine, but there have also been sticks found to contain high levels of cardboard and even paint residues. Choose a product whose ingredients are clearly described.

Overweight?

Recent investigations have shown that many dogs are overweight. A dog usually gets too fat because of over-feeding and lack of exercise. Use of medicines or a disease is rarely the cause. Dogs that get too fat are often given too much food or too many treats between meals. Gluttony or boredom can also be a cause, and a dog often puts on weight following castration or sterilisation. Due to changes in hormone levels it becomes less active and consumes less energy. Finally, simply too little exercise alone can lead to a dog becoming overweight.

You can use the following rule of thumb to check whether your dog is overweight: you should be able to feel its ribs, but not see them. If you can't feel its ribs then your dog is much too fat. Overweight dogs live a passive life, they play too little and tire quickly. They also suffer from all kinds of medical problems (problems in joints and heart conditions). They usually die younger too.

So it's important to make sure that your dog doesn't get too fat. Always follow the guidelines on food packaging. Adapt them if your dog is less active or gets lots of snacks. Try to make sure that your dog gets plenty of exercise by playing and running with it as much as possible. If your dog starts to show signs of putting on weight you can switch to a low-calorie food. If it's really too fat and reducing the quantity of its food doesn't help, then a special diet is the only solution.

Caring for your Shih Tzu

Good (daily) care is extremely important for your dog. A well cared for dog is less likely to become ill. Caring for your dog is not only necessary but also a pleasure.

Master and dog are giving each other some attention, and it's an excellent opportunity for a game and a cuddle.

The coat

Caring for your dog's coat involves regular brushing and combing, together with checking for parasites such as fleas, mites or ticks. Shih Tzu need a considerable amount of grooming. How often a dog needs to be brushed and combed depends on its type of coat. Brushing removes dead hairs and spreads body oil throughout the whole coat. Check your Shih Tzu for tangles behind the ears, legs, in its groin and breech. These are best removed by brushing them out. If a tangle is too big, separate it carefully with your fingers and then comb and

brush out – avoid scissoring as it damages the coat badly.

Brush your dog thoroughly twice a week. Never work on a dry coat – spray it with hair conditioner or even water before you start brushing. First free up the coat with a stiff brush (rigorously like a massage), layer after layer, and then comb it until all tangles are gone. After that, brush it again with a soft brush to spread the fat and finish by parting the coat along the spine. When you've finished brushing, tie the hair on the top of the head into a neat topknot with a soft rubber band.

Use the right equipment for taking care of the coat. A stiff brush, a soft brush, a medium to fine comb and a fine flea brush (preferably not plastic) will do.

Combs should not be too sharp. Always brush and comb from the head back towards the tail, following the direction of the hair. Additionally, beard and whiskers should be cleaned, preferably every day – rinse them with warm water, dry with a cloth and comb.

Profuse hair between the soles of the feet should be kept short. This is more pleasant for the dog, otherwise it 'slides' on these hairs and collects particles of soil and dirt, making walking unpleasant.

If you get a puppy used to being brushed from an early age, it will enjoy having its coat cared for. A Shih Tzu should be bathed from time to time. Always use a special dog shampoo and make sure it doesn't get into the dog's eyes or ears. Rinse the suds out thoroughly. A vet can prescribe special medicinal shampoos for some skin conditions. Always follow the instructions to the letter. After bathing use a hair-dryer and brush until your dog is dry and its coat is free of tangles. Never let a dog dry by itself. Make sure your Shih Tzu is completely dry before letting it outdoors again. Even dogs can catch a cold!

Good flea prevention is highly important to avoid skin and coat problems. Fleas must be treated not only on the dog itself but also in its surroundings (see the

chapter Parasites). Coat problems can also occur due to an allergy to certain food substances. In such cases, a vet can prescribe a hypoallergenic diet.

If you feel unable to cope with frequent and prolonged grooming sessions, it's better to have your Shih Tzu clipped by a professional dog groomer rather than the coat being neglected and becoming tangled. This does not mean that a clipped dog doesn't require grooming, but it is considerably simpler and easier. A vigorous brush once a week will usually suffice.

Teeth

A dog must be able to eat properly to stay in good condition, so it needs healthy teeth. Check

Nails

If a dog regularly walks on hard surfaces, its nails usually grind themselves down. In this case there's no need to clip their nails. But it wouldn't do any harm to check their length now and again, especially on dogs that don't get out on the streets often. Using a piece of paper, you can easily see whether its nails are too long. If you can push the paper between the nail and the ground when the dog is standing, then the nail is the right length.

Nails that are too long may bother your dog. It can injure itself when scratching, so they must be kept trimmed. You can buy special nail clippers in pet shops. Be careful not to clip back too far as you could cut into the quick, which can bleed profusely. If you feel unsure, have this necessary task done by a vet or an animal beauty parlour.

its teeth regularly. Get in touch with your vet if you suspect that all is not well. Regular feeds of hard dry food can help keep your dog's teeth clean and healthy. There are special dog chews on the market that help prevent tartar and help keep the animal's breath fresh.

What really helps is to regularly brush your dog's teeth. You can use special toothbrushes for dogs, but a finger wrapped in a small piece of gauze will also do the job. Get your dog used to having its teeth cleaned at an early age and you won't have problems.

You can even teach an older dog to have its teeth cleaned. With a dog chew as a reward it will certainly be happy.

Eyes

A dog's eyes should be cleaned and rinsed (preferably with normal saline solution) every day. 'Sleepies' and little lumps of dried eye moisture can get into the corners of the eye. You can easily remove them by wiping them downward with your thumb. If you don't like doing that, use a dry piece of tissue or toilet paper.

Keeping your dog's eyes clean will take only a few seconds a day, so do it every day. If the sleepies become yellow and slimy, this points to heavy irritation or an infection. When the eyelids are red, it's a sign of an infection which is best taken care of by your vet. Eye drops or ointment will quickly solve this problem.

Ears

The ears are often forgotten when caring for dogs, but they must be checked at least once a week. If its ears are very dirty or have too much wax, you must clean them. This should preferably be done with a clean cotton cloth, which is moistened with baby oil. Cotton wool is not suitable due to the fluff it can leave behind. NEVER penetrate the ear canal with an object.

If hairs inside the ears cause problems, then it's best to remove them. Carefully pull them out using your thumb and index finger.

If you neglect cleaning your dog's ears there's a substantial risk of infection. A dog that is constantly scratching at its ears might be suffering from dirty ears, an ear infection or ear mites, making a visit to the vet essential.

Bringing up
your Shih T:

**It is very important that
your dog is properly
brought up and obedient.
Not only will this bring you
more pleasure, but it's also
nicer for your environment.**

A puppy can learn what it may
and may not do in a playful
manner. Rewards and consistency
are important tools when bringing
up a dog. Reward it with your
voice, a pat or something tasty,
and it will quickly learn to obey. A
puppy training course can also
help you along the way.

(Dis)obedience

A dog that won't obey you is not
just a problem for you, but also for
your surroundings. It's therefore
important to avoid unwanted
behaviour. In fact, this is what
training your dog is all about, so
get started early. 'Start 'em
young!' applies to dogs too. An
untrained dog is not just a
nuisance, but can also cause
dangerous situations by running
onto the street, chasing joggers or

jumping at people. A dog must be
trained out of this undesirable
behaviour as quickly as possible.
The longer you let it go on, the
more difficult it will become to
correct. The best thing to do is to
attend a special obedience course.
This won't only help to correct the
dog's behaviour, but its owner also
learns how to handle undesirable
behaviour at home. A dog must
not only obey its master during
training, but at home too.

Always be consistent when
training good behaviour and
correcting annoying behaviour.
This means a dog may always
behave in a certain way, or must
never behave that way. Reward it
for good behaviour and never
punish it after the event for any
wrongdoing. If your dog finally

comes after you've been calling it a long time, then reward it. If you're angry because you had to wait so long, it may feel it's actually being punished for coming. It will probably not obey at all the next time for fear of punishment.

Try to take no notice of undesirable behaviour. Your dog will perceive your reaction (even a negative one) as a reward for this behaviour. If you need to correct the dog, then do this immediately. Use your voice or grip it by the scruff of its neck and push it to the ground. This is the way a mother dog calls her pups to order. Rewards for good behaviour are, by far, preferable to punishment; they always achieve a better result.

House-training

The very first training (and one of the most important) that a dog needs is house-training. The basis for good house-training is keeping a good eye on your puppy. If you pay attention, you will notice that it will sniff a long time and turn around a certain spot before doing its business there. Pick it up gently and place it outdoors, always at the same spot. Reward it abundantly if it does its business there.

Another good moment for house-training is after eating or sleeping. A puppy often needs to do its business at these times. Let it

relieve itself before playing with it, otherwise it will forget to do so and you'll not reach your goal. For the first few days, take your puppy out for a walk just after it's eaten or woken up. It will quickly learn the meaning, especially if it's rewarded with a dog biscuit for a successful attempt. Of course, it's not always possible to go out after every snack or snooze. Lay newspapers at different spots in the house. Whenever your pup needs to do its business, place it on a newspaper. After some time it will start to look for a place itself. Then start to reduce the number of newspapers until there is just one left, at the front or back door. The

First exercises

The basic commands for an obedient dog are those for sit, lie down, come and stay. But a puppy should first learn its name. Use it as much as possible from the first day on followed by a friendly 'Come!'. Reward it with your voice and a pat when it comes to you. Your puppy will quickly understand your intention and has now learned its first command in a playful manner. Don't appear too strict towards a young puppy, and don't always punish it immediately if it doesn't react in the right way. When you call your puppy to you in this way, have it come right to you. You can teach a pup to sit by holding a piece of dog biscuit above its nose and then slowly moving it backwards. The puppy's head will also move backwards until its hind legs slowly go down. At that moment you call 'Sit!'. After a few attempts, it will quickly get the hang of this nice game. Use the 'Sit!' command before you give your dog its food, put it on the lead, or before it's allowed to cross the street.

puppy will learn to go to the door if it needs to relieve itself. Then you put it on the lead and go out with it. Finally you can remove the last newspaper. Your puppy is now house-trained.

One thing that certainly won't work is punishing an accident after the event. A dog whose nose is rubbed in its urine or its droppings won't understand that at all. It will only get frightened of you. Rewarding works much better than punishment. An indoor kennel or cage can be a good tool to help in house-training. A puppy won't foul its own nest, so a kennel can be a good solution for the night, or during periods in the day when you can't watch it. But a kennel must not become a prison where your dog is locked up day and night.

Teaching the command to lie down is similar. Instead of moving the piece of dog biscuit backwards, move it down vertically until your hand reaches the ground and then forwards. The dog will also move its forepaws forwards and lie down on its own. At that moment call 'Lie down!'

or 'Lay!'. This command is useful when you want a dog to be quiet.

Two people are needed for the 'Come!' command. One holds the dog back while the other runs away. After about fifteen metres, he stops and enthusiastically calls 'Come!'. The other person now lets the dog free, and it should obey the command at once. Again you reward it abundantly. The 'Come!' command is useful in many situations and good for safety too. This is a particularly important command for any dog, otherwise your companion may be condemned to always being walked on the lead.

A dog learns to stay from the sitting or lying position. While it's sitting or lying down, you call the command 'Stay!' and then step back one step. If the dog moves with you, quietly put it back in position, without displaying anger. If you react angrily, you're actually punishing it for coming to you, and you'll only confuse your dog. It can't understand that coming is rewarded one time, and punished another. Once your dog stays nicely, reward it abundantly. Practise this exercise with increasing distances (at first no more than one metre). The 'Stay!' command is useful when getting out of the car.

Courses

Obedience courses to help you bring up your dog are available across the country. These courses are not just informative, but also fun for dog and master.

With a puppy, you can begin with a puppy course. This is designed to provide the basic training. A puppy that has attended such a course has learned about all kinds of things that will confront it in later life: other dogs, humans, traffic and what these mean. The puppy will also learn obedience and to follow a number of basic commands. Apart from all that, attention will be given to important subjects such as brushing, being alone, travelling in a car, and doing its business in the right places.

The next step after a puppy course is a course for young dogs. This course repeats the basic exercises and ensures that the growing dog doesn't learn bad habits. After this, your dog can move on to an obedience course for full-grown dogs. For more information on where to find courses in your area, contact your local kennel club. You can get its address from the Kennel Club of Great Britain in London. In some areas, the RSPCA organises obedience classes and your local branch may be able to give you information.

Play and toys

There are various ways to play with your dog. You can romp and run with it, but also play a number of games, such as retrieving, tug-of-war, hide-and-seek and catch. A tennis ball is ideal for retrieving; you can play tug-of-war with an old sock or a special tugging rope. Start with tug-of-war only when your dog is a year old. A puppy must first get its second teeth and then they need several months to strengthen. There's a real chance of your dog's teeth becoming deformed if you start too young. It is also very important that you always win the game – it should end only when you decide so and the toy is in your possession. You can use almost anything for a game of hide-and-seek. A frisbee is ideal for catching games. Never use too small a ball for games. It can easily get lodged in your dog's throat.

Play is extremely important. Not only does it strengthen the bond between dog and master, but it's also healthy for both. Make sure that you're the one that ends the game. Only stop when your dog has brought back the ball or frisbee. This confirms your dominant position in the hierarchy. Use these toys only during play so that your dog doesn't forget their significance. When choosing a special dog toy, remember that dogs are rarely careful with them. So always buy toys of good quality that a dog can't easily destroy.

Be very careful with sticks and twigs. The latter, in particular, can easily splinter. A splinter of wood in your dog's throat or intestines can cause awful problems. Throwing sticks or twigs can also be dangerous. If they stick into the ground a dog can easily run into them with an open mouth.

Aggression

A Shih Tzu should never appear aggressive. But even they can sometimes be quite bossy and difficult with other animals or people, so it's good to understand more about the background of aggression in dogs.

There are two different types of aggressive behaviour: The anxious-aggressive dog and the

The dominant-aggressive dog's body language is different. It walks on straight legs and its tail is raised and stiff. This dog will always go for its victim's arms, legs or throat. It is extremely self-assured and highly placed in the dog hierarchy. Its attack is a display of power rather than a consequence of fear. This dog needs to know who's boss. You must bring it up rigorously and with a strong hand. An obedience course can help. Fortunately, this type of aggressive behaviour is rare with Shih Tzu.

dominant-aggressive dog. An anxious-aggressive dog can be recognised by its pulled back ears and its low posture. It will have pulled in its lips, baring its teeth. This dog is aggressive because it's very frightened and feels cornered. It would prefer to run away, but if it can't then it will bite to defend itself. It will grab its victim anywhere it can. The attack is usually brief and, as soon as the dog can see a way to escape, it's gone. In a confrontation with other dogs, it will normally turn out as the loser. It can become even more aggressive once it's realised that people or other dogs are afraid of it. This behaviour cannot be corrected just like that. First you have to try and understand what the dog is afraid of. Professional advice is a good idea here because the wrong approach can easily make the problem worse.

A dog may also bite itself because it's in pain. This is a natural defensive reaction. In this case try to resolve the dog's fear as far as possible. Reward it for letting you get to the painful spot. Be careful, because a dog in pain may also bite its master! In case you have to do anything that might be painful, grab your dog firmly by the scruff of its neck, so that it can't bite, and talk to it softly. Never punish a dog for this type of aggression!

Fear
The source of anxious behaviour can often be traced to the first weeks of a dog's life. A shortage of new experiences during this important phase (also called the 'socialisation phase') has great influence on its later behaviour. A dog that never encountered humans, other dogs or animals during the socialisation phase will

be afraid of them later. This fear is common in dogs brought up in a barn or kennel, with almost no contact with humans. As we saw, fear can lead to aggressive behaviour, so it's important that a puppy gets as many new impressions as possible in the first weeks of its life. Take it with you into town in the car or on the bus, walk it down busy streets and allow it to have plenty of contact with people, other dogs and other animals.

It's a huge task to turn an anxious, poorly socialised dog into a real pet. It will probably take an enormous amount of attention, love, patience and energy to get such an animal used to everything around it. Reward it often and give it plenty of time to adapt and, over time, it will learn to trust you and become less anxious. Try not to force anything, because that will always have the reverse effect. Here too, an obedience course can help a lot. A dog can be especially afraid of strangers. Have visitors give it something tasty as a treat. Put a can of dog biscuits by the door so that your visitors can spoil your dog when they arrive. Here again, don't try to force anything. If the dog is still frightened, leave it in peace.

Dogs are often frightened in certain situations; well-known examples are thunderstorms and fireworks. In these cases try to ignore their anxious behaviour. If you react to their whimpering and whining, it's the same as rewarding it. If you ignore its fear completely, the dog will quickly learn that nothing is wrong. You can speed up this 'learning process' by rewarding positive behaviour.

Rewarding
Rewarding forms the basis for bringing up a dog. Rewarding good behaviour works far better than punishing bad behaviour and rewarding is also much more fun. Over time the opinions on bringing up dogs have gradually changed. In the past the proper way to correct bad behaviour was a sharp pull on the lead. Today,

experts regard rewards as a positive incentive to get dogs to do what we expect of them. There are many ways to reward a dog. The usual ways are a pat or a friendly word, even without a tasty treat to go with it. Of course, a piece of dog biscuit does wonders when you're training a puppy. Be sure you always have something delicious in your pocket to reward good behaviour. Another form of reward is play. Whenever a dog notices that you have a ball in your pocket, it won't go far from your side. As soon as you've finished playing, put the ball away. This way your dog will always do its best in exchange for a game.

Despite the emphasis you put on rewarding good behaviour, a dog can sometimes be a nuisance or disobedient. You must correct such behaviour immediately. Always be consistent: once 'no' must always be 'no'.

Barking

Dogs which bark too much are often a nuisance for their surroundings. A dog owner may tolerate barking up to a certain point, but neighbours are often annoyed by the unnecessary noise. Shih Tzu are not particularly noisy, so don't encourage your puppy to bark and yelp. Of course, it should be able to announce its presence, but if it goes on barking it must be called to order with a strict 'Quiet!'. If a puppy fails to obey, just hold its muzzle closed with your hand.

A dog will sometimes bark for long periods when left alone. It feels threatened and tries to get someone's attention by barking. There are special training programmes for this problem, where dogs learn that being alone is nothing to be afraid of, and that its master will always return.

You can practise this with your dog at home. Leave the room and come back in at once. Reward your dog if it stays quiet. Gradually increase the length of your absences and keep rewarding it as long as it remains quiet. Never punish your dog if it does bark or yelp. It will never understand punishment afterwards, and this will only make the problem worse. Never go back into the room as long as your dog is barking, as it will view this as a reward. You might want to make the dog feel more comfortable by switching the radio on for company during your absence. It will eventually learn that you always come back and the barking will reduce. If you don't get the required result, attend an obedience course.

Reproductio

Dogs, and thus also Shih Tzu, follow their instincts, and reproduction is one of nature's important processes. For people who enjoy breeding dogs this is a positive circumstance.

Those who simply want a cosy companion, however, will miss the regular adventures with females on heat and unrestrainable males like a hole in the head. But knowing a little about canine reproduction will help you to understand why they behave the way they do, and what measures you need to take when this happens.

Liability

Breeding dogs is much more than simply 1+1= many. If you're planning to breed from your Shih Tzu bitch, be on your guard, otherwise the whole affair can turn into a (financial) drama, as, according to the law, a breeder is liable for the 'quality' of his puppies.

The kennel clubs place strict conditions on animals used for breeding. They must be examined for possible congenital defects (see the chapter Your Shih Tzu's health). This is the breeder's first obligation, and if you breed a litter and sell the puppies without these checks having been made, you can be held liable by the new owners for any costs arising from any inherited defects. These (veterinary) costs can be enormous! So contact the breed association if you plan to breed a litter of Shih Tzu.

The female in season

Bitches become sexually mature at about eight to twelve months. Then they go into season for the first time. They are 'on heat' for two to three weeks. During this period they discharge little drops of blood and they are very attractive to males. The bitch is fertile during the second half of her season, and will accept a male to mate. The best time for mating is generally between the tenth and thirteenth day of her season. A female's first season is often shorter and less severe than those that follow. If you do want to breed from your female, you must allow this first (and preferably also the second) season to pass. Most bitches go into season twice per year. If you do plan to breed from your Shih Tzu in the future, then sterilisation is not an option to prevent unwanted offspring. A temporary solution is a contraceptive injection, although this is controversial because of serious side effects such as womb inflammation (pyometra).

Phantom pregnancy

A phantom pregnancy is a not uncommon occurrence with Shih Tzu. The female behaves as if she has a litter. She takes all kinds of things to her basket and treats them like puppies. Her milk teats swell up and sometimes milk is actually produced. The female will sometimes behave aggressively towards people or other animals, as if she is defending her young.

Phantom pregnancies usually begin two months after a season and can last a number of weeks. If it happens to a bitch once, it will often then occur after every season. If she suffers under it, sterilisation

is the best solution, because continual phantom pregnancies increase the risk of womb or teat conditions. In the short term a hormone treatment is worth trying, perhaps also homeopathic medicines. Camphor spirit can give relief when teats are heavily swollen, but rubbing the teats with ice or a cold cloth (moisten and freeze) can also help relieve the pain. Feed the female less than usual, and makes sure she gets enough distraction and extra exercise.

Preparing to breed

If you do plan to breed a litter of puppies, you must first wait for your female to be physically and mentally full-grown. In any event you must let her first season pass. To mate a bitch, you need a male. You could simply let her out on the street and she would quickly return home pregnant. But if you have a pure-bred Shih Tzu, then it certainly makes sense to mate her with the best possible candidate, even if she has no pedigree. Proceed with caution and think especially about the following:

• Accompanying a bitch through pregnancy, birth and the first eight to twelve weeks afterwards is a time consuming affair.
• Never breed from dogs that have congenital defects, and this also applies to dogs without papers. The same goes for hyperactive, nervous and shy dogs.

• If your Shih Tzu does have a pedigree, then mate her with a dog that also has one. For more information, contact the breed association.

Pregnancy

It's often difficult to tell at first whether a bitch is pregnant. Only after about four weeks can you feel the pups in her belly. She will now slowly get fatter and her behaviour will usually change. Her teats will swell during the last few weeks of pregnancy. The average pregnancy lasts 63 days, and costs her a lot of energy.

In the beginning she is fed her normal amount of food, but her nutritional needs increase in jumps during the second half of the pregnancy. Give her approximately fifteen percent more food each week from the fifth week on. The mother-to-be needs extra energy and proteins during this phase of her pregnancy. During the last weeks you can give her a concentrated food, rich in energy, such as dry puppy food. Divide this into several small portions per day, because she can no longer deal with large portions of food. Towards the end of the pregnancy, her energy needs can easily be one-and-a-half times more than usual.

After about seven weeks the mother will start to demonstrate nesting behaviour and to look for a place to give birth to her young. This might be her own basket or a special birthing box. This must be ready at

least a week before the birth to give the mother time to get used to it. The basket or box should preferably be in a quiet, draught-free place.

The birth

The average litter is four or five puppies. The birth usually passes without problems, but one has to be aware that - due to the relatively large heads of the puppies - difficulties may occur. Stay in touch with a vet and contact him immediately if you suspect a problem!

Suckling

After giving birth, the mother starts to produce milk. The suckling period is very demanding. During the first three to four weeks the pups rely entirely on their mother's milk. During this time she needs extra food and fluids. This can be up to three or four times the normal amount. If she's producing too little milk, you can give both mother and her young special puppy milk. Here too, divide the high quantity of food the mother needs over several smaller portions. Again, choose a concentrated, high-energy, food and give her plenty of fresh drinking water, but not cow milk, as this can cause diarrhoea.

You can give the puppies some supplemental solid food when they are three to four weeks old. There are special puppy foods available that follow on well from the

mother's milk and can easily be eaten with their milk teeth.

Ideally, the puppies are fully weaned at an age of seven or eight weeks, i.e. they no longer drink their mother's milk. The mother's milk production gradually stops and her food needs also drop. Within a couple of weeks after weaning, the mother should be getting the same amount of food as before the pregnancy again.

Castration and sterilisation

As soon as you are sure that your bitch should never bear a (new) litter, a vasectomy or sterilisation is the best solution. During sterilisation (in fact this is the same as castration) the uterus and ovaries are surgically removed. The bitch no longer goes into season and can never become pregnant. The best age for a sterilisation is about eighteen months, when the bitch is more or less fully grown.

A male dog is usually only castrated for medical reasons or to correct undesirable sexual behaviour. During a castration the testicles are removed, which is a simple procedure and usually without complications. There is no required age for castration, but, if possible, wait until the dog is fully grown. Vasectomy is sufficient where it's only a case of making the dog infertile. In this case the dog keeps its sexual drive but can no longer reproduce.

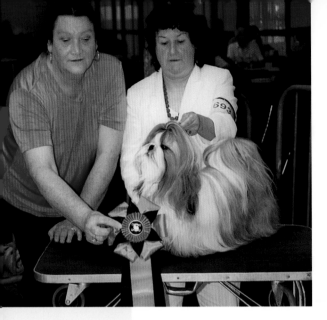

Shows

Visiting a dog show is a pleasant experience for both dog and master, and for some dog-lovers it has become a hobby. They visit countless shows every year.

Exhibitions and exemption shows

Visiting a dog show is a special experience for both dog and master, and for some dog-lovers it is an intensive hobby. They visit countless shows every year. Others find it nice to visit an exemption show with their dog just once. It's worth making the effort to visit an exemption show where a judge's trained eyes will inspect your Shih Tzu and assess it for form, gait, condition and type. The judge's report will teach you your dog's weak and strong points, which may help you when choosing a mate for breeding. You can also exchange experiences with other Shih Tzu owners. Official exemption shows are only open to dogs with a recognised pedigree.

Ring training

If you've never been to an exemption show, you're probably tapping in the dark in terms of what will be expected of you and your dog. Many kennel clubs organise so-called ring training courses for dogs going to an exemption show for the first time. This training teaches you exactly what the judge will be looking for, and you can practise this together with your dog.

Club matches

Almost all kennel clubs organise club matches. You must register your dog in a certain class in advance. These meetings are often small and friendly and are usually the first acquaintance a dog and its master make with a judge. This is an overwhelming experience for your dog - a lot of its contemporaries and a stranger

who fiddles around with it and peers into its mouth. After a few times, your dog will know exactly what's expected of it.

Championship shows

Various championship shows take place during the course of the year with different prizes. These shows are much more strictly organised than club matches. Your dog must be registered in a certain class in advance and it will then be listed in a catalogue. On the day itself, the dog is kept on a bench until its turn comes up. During the judging in the ring, it's important that you show your dog at its best. The judge gives an official verdict and issues a report. When all the dogs from that class have been judged, the best are selected. After the judging for that breed is finished, you can pick up your report and any prize you may have won. The winners of the various classes then compete for the title Best of Breed where a winner is chosen from all the dogs in the same breed group. Finally, the winners of each breed group compete for the title of Best of Group and, finally, Best in Show.

Of course, your dog must look very smart for the show. The judge will not be impressed if its coat is not clean or if it is tangled, and if its paws are dirty. Nails must be clipped, eyes and teeth clean. The dog must also be free of parasites and ailments. It is advisable for a Shih Tzu to be bathed a few days, or even a day, before the show. A bitch must not be in season and a male must be in possession of both testicles. Apart from those things, judges do not value badly brought-up, anxious or nervous dogs. Get in touch with your local dog club or the breed association if you want to know more about shows.

Don't forget!

If you're planning to take your dog to a club match or show, you need to be well prepared. Remember to take the following:

For yourself:
- Registration card
- Food and drink
- Safety pin for the catalogue number
- Chair(s)

For your dog:
- Food and drink bowls and food
- Dog blanket and perhaps a cushion
- Show lead
- Grooming equipment

Parasites

All dogs are vulnerable to various sorts of parasites. Parasites are tiny creatures that live at the expense of another animal. They feed on blood, skin and other body substances.

There are two main types. Internal parasites live within their host animal's body (tapeworm and roundworm) and external parasites live on the body surface, usually in the dog's coat (fleas and ticks), but also in its ears (ear mite).

Fleas

Fleas feed on a dog's blood. They not only cause itching and skin problems, but they can also carry infections, such as tapeworm. In large numbers they can cause anaemia, and dogs can also become allergic to a flea's saliva, which can cause serious skin conditions. So it's important to treat your dog for fleas as effectively as possible, not just on the dog itself but also in its surroundings. For treatment on the animal, there are various medicines: drops for the neck and to put in its food, flea collars, long-life sprays and flea powders. You can find various sprays in pet shops, which can be used to eradicate fleas in the dog's immediate surroundings. Choose a spray that kills both adult fleas and their larvae. If your dog goes in your car, you should spray that too.

Fleas can also affect other pets, so you should treat those too. When spraying a room, cover any aquarium or fishbowl. If the spray reaches the water, it can be fatal for your fish! Switch off the oxygen pump for an hour. During and directly after spraying the room, no pets are allowed in there. To protect yourself, you should

Flea

cover your mouth and nose.
Your vet and pet shop have a wide
range of flea treatments and can
advise you on the subject.

Ticks

Ticks are small, spider-like
parasites. They feed on the blood
of the animal or person they've
settled on. A tick looks like a tiny,
grey-coloured leather bag with
eight legs. When it has sucked
itself full, it can easily be five to
ten times its own size and it is

darker in colour.
Dogs usually become victims to
ticks in bushes, woods or long
grass. Ticks cause not only
irritation by sucking their blood,
but they can also carry a number
of serious diseases. This applies
especially to the Mediterranean
countries, which can be infested
with blood parasites. In our
country these diseases are
fortunately less common.
Unfortunately Lyme disease,
which can also affect humans, has

Left: Full tick
Right: In normal
condition

reached our shores. Your vet can prescribe a special treatment if you're planning to take your dog to southern Europe. It is important to fight ticks as effectively as possible. Check your dog regularly, especially when it has been running free in woods and shrubs. It can also wear an anti-tick collar.

Removing a tick is simple using a tick pincette. Grip the tick with the pincette, as close to the dog's skin as possible, and carefully pull it out. You can also grip the tick between your fingers and, using a turning movement, carefully pull it out. You must disinfect the spot where the tick was attached, using iodine to prevent infection. Never soak the tick in alcohol, ether or oil. In a shock reaction the tick may discharge the infected contents of its stomach into your dog's skin.

Ear mites

Itchy ears are sometimes a symptom of ear mites – small parasites that cause severe irritation and are easily passed from dog to dog (and to cats). Treatment should start with the vet carefully clearing away the wax from inside the ear, followed by application of a prescribed medicine. All animals in the household must be treated at the same time.

Worms

Dogs can suffer from various types of worms. The most common are tapeworm and roundworm. Tapeworm causes diarrhoea and poor condition. If your dog is suffering from a tapeworm infection, you can sometimes find small pieces of the worm around the dog's anus or on its bed. In this case, the dog must be wormed. You should also check your dog for fleas, which may carry a tapeworm infection.

Tapeworms

Roundworm is a condition that reoccurs regularly. Puppies are often infected in their mother's womb. Roundworm causes problems (particularly in younger dogs), such as diarrhoea, loss of weight and poor growth. In serious cases the pup becomes thin, but with a swollen belly. It may vomit and you can then see the worms in its vomit. They are spaghetti-like tendrils.

A puppy must be treated for worms regularly with a worm treatment. Adult dogs should be treated every six months.

Roundworms

Your Shih Tzu's health

This book is too limited for u
to describe all the diseases
your dog may suffer from.
Therefore we only provide
detailed descriptions of the
conditions which are typical
of this breed or which occur
more frequently in it.

Eyes

The relatively large, frontally set
eyes of the Shih Tzu are prone
to infections and injuries. It is
inadvisable to walk a Shih Tzu
in the woods and through high
grass. After each walk carefully
check your dog's eyes for the
presence of seeds or stalks.
Additionally, its eyes must be
rinsed daily with a normal saline
solution (physiological salt
solution). In case of any
irritation and/or excessive
discharge get your vet to check
it out straight away.

Cataracts

This condition causes a clouding
of the cornea. You can notice it
when your dog's eye is of any
colour other than green when
seen in an artificial light.

Cataracts can be hereditary and
appear in young animals,
sometimes as early as at eight
weeks; it is passed on by both
parents. More frequently, it is
the result of an injury or another
disease. An ophthalmoscopic
examination by a qualified vet
can determine the type of
cataract. Dogs with hereditary
cataracts should not be used for
breeding.

Cleft palate

Although it is rare, it may
happen that a puppy is born with
a smaller or larger opening in its
palate. Such puppies have
difficulties suckling and – when
doing so – one can notice small
bubbles of milk coming from the
nostrils. In the most severe cases
affected puppies fade away and

die within a few days. The
condition seems to be hereditary,
but the mode of inheritance is
still unknown.

Checking the mouths of
newborn puppies should be part
of a routine veterinary
examination.

Tight nostrils

This seems to be an inherited
condition. The most severe cases
can be noticed at birth, as the
nostrils are then so tight that the
nose is deformed. Affected
puppies usually die within a few
days. Less severe cases do not
become evident until the third
week and an affected puppy
shows obvious difficulties in
breathing. It will die unless
hand-fed and kept at a
constantly high temperature.
Usually this condition lasts for
about two weeks and gradually
improves to normal.

Familial nephropathy

This is also known as kidney
dysplasia and assumed to be
hereditary, although the mode of
inheritance is yet to be
established. Whole litters can be
affected and the onset of the
disease varies from several
weeks to one year. The main
symptoms are excessive drinking
and urinating. The disease is
incurable and always fatal.

kneecap dislocates from the knee joint. A luxated kneecap can be caused by a groove that is too shallow, which is hereditary, but also by trauma (an accident). In this case the luxation may go together with torn ligaments. Luxations can occur in various grades. The amount of difficulty and pain the dog suffers varies from one dog to the other. Luxated kneecaps can be corrected surgically. Just as with larger breeds, smooth floors and unusual movements (chasing a bouncing ball, hopping and turning) are not good for the joints of smaller breeds and puppies.

Patella Luxation

In the case of this disorder, the kneecap does not sit properly on the end of the lower leg. The

Tips for the Shih Tzu owner

- A Shih Tzu is a sweet-natured dog that won't respond well to a harsh hand.
- Ignore submissive or anxious behaviour; certainly don't comfort your dog.
- A Shih Tzu can be somewhat cocky; a rigorous, but not harsh, upbringing is very important!
- Attend a puppy course with your dog. You'll both learn a thing or two.
- Visit several breeders before you buy a puppy.
- The Shih Tzu is an energetic dog. It will find dog sports great fun, but don't take them too seriously!
- Its first car journey is quite an experience for your puppy. Make sure it's a pleasant one.
- Check your Shih Tzu's coat for tangles regularly. Regularly give your dog a thorough brush!
- Don't only fight fleas, but also the larvae.
- Taking your dog on vacation? Why not?
- Hard chunks and enough to chew on keep your dog's teeth healthy.
- Never buy a puppy if you weren't able to see its mother.
- Clean your dog's eyes every day.
- A puppy is a lot of work, and can cause some grey hairs.
- Buy a Shih Tzu via the breed association.
- Make sure your dog doesn't become too fat. Not too much to eat and plenty of exercise is the golden rule.

The Shih Tzu on the internet

A great deal of information can be found on the internet. A selection of websites with interesting details and links to other sites and pages is listed here. Sometimes pages move to another site or address. You can find more sites by using the available search engines.

www.shih-tzu.se
A very interesting site, unfortunately only in Swedish, but with a remarkable list of links, see below.
• American Shih Tzu Club
• Australian Shih Tzu Club of Victoria
• Belgian Shih Tzu Club
• Canadian Shih Tzu Club
• Internationaler Shih-Tzu Club e.V. Tysk Shih Tzu kl.
• Isländska Shih Tzu
• Italienska sällskapshundklubben
- Klubcanicompagnia Italy
• Shih-Tzu Club Nederland
• T he Northern Counties Shih Tzu Club - GB
• Philippine Shih Tzu Club
• Shih Tzu Club of Scotland
• The Shih Tzu Club - UK
• Shih Tzu Club of Southeastern Wisconsin USA
• Shih Tzu Fanciers of Southern CA
• Singapore Shih Tzu Club
• Sällskapshundklubben DK
• Thailand Shih Tzu Club

www.shihtzu.index.18
A long list of links concerning breeders, clubs, crossbreeds, cutting hair, rescue, eye problems, health issues, pictures, pups for sale, Shih Tzu topknot, rescue foundation and lots more.

www.the-kennelclub.org.uk
The Kennel Club's primary objective is to promote, in every way, the general improvement of dogs. This site aims to provide you with information you may need to be a responsible pet owner and to help you keep your dog happy, safe and content.

www.pet-insurance-uk.me.uk
Find low cost pet insurance via this UK pet insurance directory.

www.pethealthcare.co.uk.
At pethealthcare.co.uk they believe that a healthy pet is a happy pet. Which is why they've brought together leading experts to create a comprehensive online source of pet care information.

www.onlinepetcare.co.uk
www.onlinepetcare.co.uk was launched in 2001 and contains information about and links to businesses and charities in the Midlands area involved in the care and purchasing of domestic animals.

www.mypetstop.com
An international, multilingual website with information on keeping, breeding, behaviour, health-related issues and much more.

www.champdogs.co.uk
Search the champ dogs database for kennels, stud dogs and litters.

www.dogtraining.co.uk
Your central resource for dog training, boarding kennels & vets in the UK.

www.k9magazine.com
This refreshing magazine is produced with today's conscientious dog owner in mind and provides a fascinating insight into the latest news, views and gossip from the UK and global dog scene, as well as an easy access point to valuable advice, tips and expert opinions from some of the world's leading pet authorities.

www.rspca.org.uk
The Royal Society for the Prevention of Cruelty to Animals. If you are interested in re-homing a dog (or another pet), pay a visit to your local RSPCA pet shelter. This site provides information on animal care.

www.waltham.com
Waltham is a firm specialized in pet care and nutrition. On this website you can find more information on pet care, training and diets.

www.aboutpets.info
The website of the publisher of the About Pets book series. An overview of the titles, availability in which languages and where in the world the books are sold.

Breed associations

Becoming a member of a breed association can be very useful for good advice and interesting activities. If the details in this book are no longer accurate, you can get the right details from the Kennel Club.

Shih Tzu Club
Secretary: Ms G Gilkes
Tel No: for further information
contact the Kennel Club

Shih Tzu Club of Scotland
Secretary: Mr Martin
Tel No: 0141 424 0160

**Shih Tzu Club of South Wales
and Western Counties**
Secretary: Miss W Rewbury
Tel No: 01823 335860

Kennel Clubs of Great Britain
The Kennel Club
1 Clarges Street
London UK
WIJ 8AB
Tel: 0870 606 6750
Fax: 020 7518 1058
www.the-kennelclub.org.uk

Manchu Shih Tzu Society
Secretary: Mrs V Goodwin
Tel No: 01795 830247

**Northern Counties Shih Tzu
Club**
Secretary: Ms Buchanan
Tel No: 01254 388510

The Scottish Kennel Club
Eskmills Park
Station Road
Musselborough EH 21 7 PQ
Tel: 0131 665 3920
Fax: 0131 653 6937
Email:
info@scottishkennelclub.org
www.scottishkennelclub.org

The Irish Kennel Club Ltd.
Fottrell House
Harold's Cross Bridge
Dublin 6W
Ireland
Tel: (01) 4533300 – 4532309 -
4532310
Fax: (01) 4533237
Email: ikenclub@indigo.ie
www.ikc.ie/

The Shih Tzu

Name:	Shih Tzu
Kennel Club Classification:	Utility group
First standard:	Great Britain, 1935
Origin:	Tibet
Original tasks:	Toy dog and companion
Character:	Full of itself, sturdy, tough. Mentally stable, not shy, not noisy. Intelligent, active, alert, kind and Independent.
Weight:	4.5 to 8.1 kgs
Average life expectancy:	Approx. 10 - 12 years

The **Shih Tzu**